W9-BKV-719

Pebble Plus

Exploremos la galaxia/Exploring the Galaxy

Neptuno/Neptune

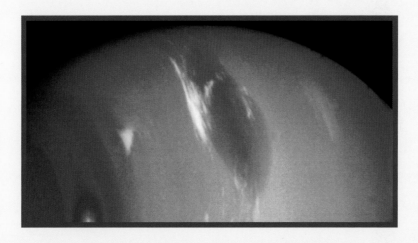

por/by Thomas K. Adamson

Traducción/Translation: Martín Luis Guzmán Ferrer, Ph.D.
Editor Consultor/Consulting Editor: Dra. Gail Saunders-Smith

James Gerard, Consultant
Aerospace Education Specialist, NASA
Kennedy Space Center, Florida

Capstone press

Mankato, Minnesota

Pebble Plus is published by Capstone Press
151 Good Counsel Drive, P.O. Box 669, Mankato, Minnesota 56002
http://www.capstone-press.com

1 2 3 4 5 6 11 10 09 08 07 06

Library of Congress Cataloging-in-Publication Data
Adamson, Thomas K.
     [Neptune. Spanish & English]
     Neptuno = Neptune / by Thomas K. Adamson.
     p. cm.—(Pebble plus: Exploremos la galaxia = Exploring the galaxy)
     English and Spanish.
     Includes index.
     ISBN-13: 978-0-7368-5882-3 (hardcover)
     ISBN-10: 0-7368-5882-2 (hardcover)
     1. Neptune (Planet)—Juvenile literature. I. Title: Neptune. II. Title. III. Series.
QB691.A3318 2005
523.48'1—dc22   2005019042

Summary: Simple text and photographs describe the planet Neptune.

Editorial Credits
Mari C. Schuh, editor; Kia Adams, designer; Alta Schaffer, photo researcher; Eida del Risco, Spanish copy editor; Jenny Marks, bilingual editor

Photo Credits
Digital Vision, 5 (Venus)
NASA, 1, 4 (Pluto), 7, 15, 17, 21; JPL, 5 (Jupiter); JPL/Caltech, 5 (Uranus), 13
PhotoDisc Inc., cover, 4 (Neptune), 5 (Mars, Mercury, Earth, Sun, Saturn), 11 (both); Stock Trek, 9, 19

Note to Parents and Teachers

The Exploremos la galaxia/Exploring the Galaxy series supports national standards related to earth and space science. This book describes Neptune in both English and Spanish. The photographs support early readers and language learners in understanding the text. Repetition of words and phrases helps early readers and language learners learn new words. This book also introduces early readers to subject-specific vocabulary words, which are defined in the Glossary section. Early readers may need assistance to read some words and to use the Table of Contents, Glossary, Internet Sites, and Index sections of the book.

Table of Contents

Tabla de contenidos

Neptune

Neptune is the eighth
planet from the Sun.
Neptune looks bright blue.

Neptuno

Neptuno es el octavo
planeta a partir del Sol.
Neptuno se ve de color
azul brillante.

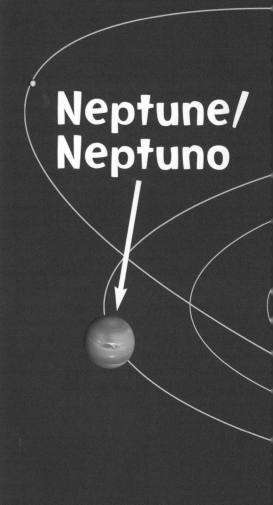

Neptune/
Neptuno

The Solar System/El sistema solar

Sun/El Sol

Clouds

Neptune is a big ball
of gases and clouds.
It is called a gas giant.

Nubes

Neptuno es una enorme
bola de gases y nubes.
Se le conoce como
un gigante gaseoso.

White clouds move across
Neptune. The clouds often
change shape.

Alrededor de Neptuno
se mueven nubes blancas. A
menudo las nubes cambian
de forma.

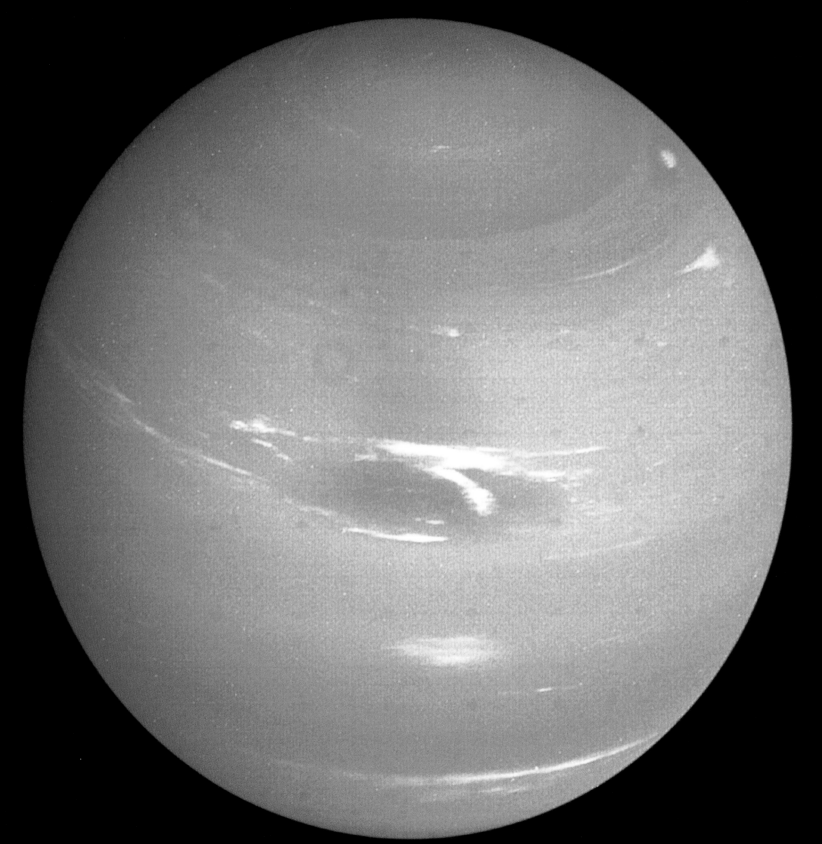

9

Neptune's Size

Neptune is the fourth largest planet. Neptune is almost four times wider than Earth.

El tamaño de Neptuno

Neptuno es el cuarto planeta más grande. Neptuno es casi cuatro veces más grande que la Tierra.

Earth/La Tierra

Neptune/Neptuno

11

Neptune's Moons

At least 11 moons move
around Neptune. Most of
the moons are small,
icy chunks of rock.

Las lunas de Neptuno

Por lo menos 11 lunas se mueven
alrededor de Neptuno. La mayoría
de estas lunas son pedazos
pequeños de roca con hielo.

13

Neptune's largest moon
is called Triton. It is
made of rock and ice.

La luna más grande de
Neptuno se llama Tritón.
Está hecha de roca y hielo.

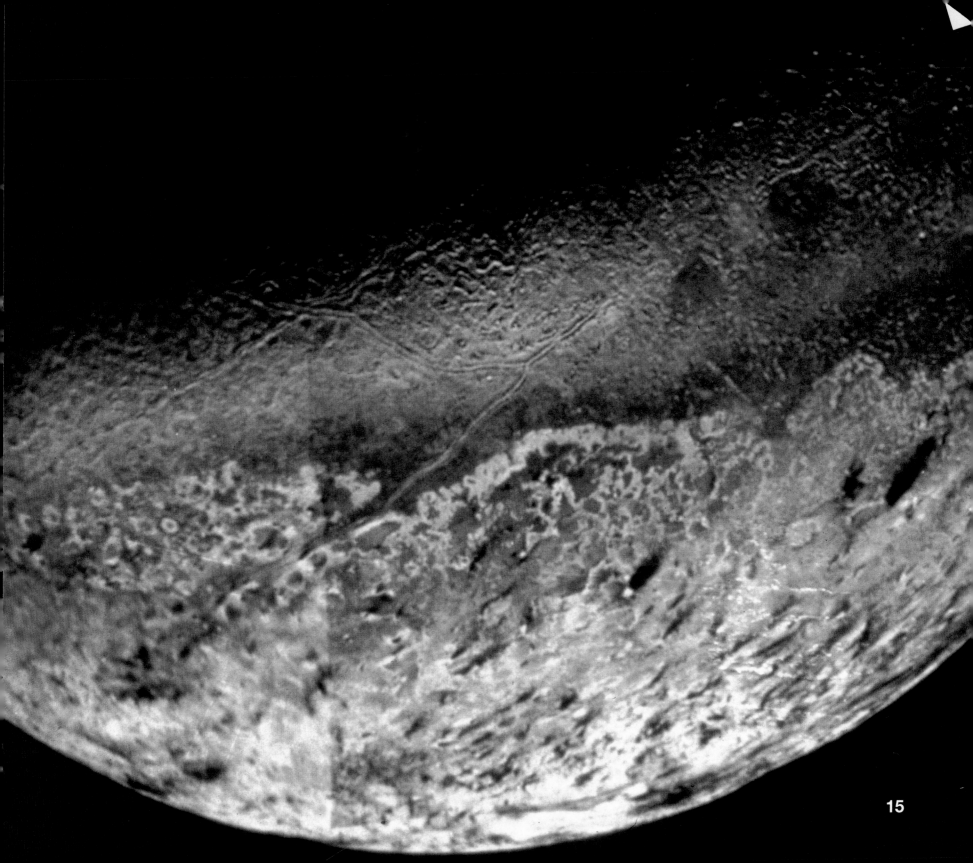

15

Triton probably looks like
the planet Pluto. Triton is
one of the coldest places
in the solar system.

Probablemente Tritón se parece
al planeta Plutón. Tritón es
uno de los lugares más fríos
del sistema solar.

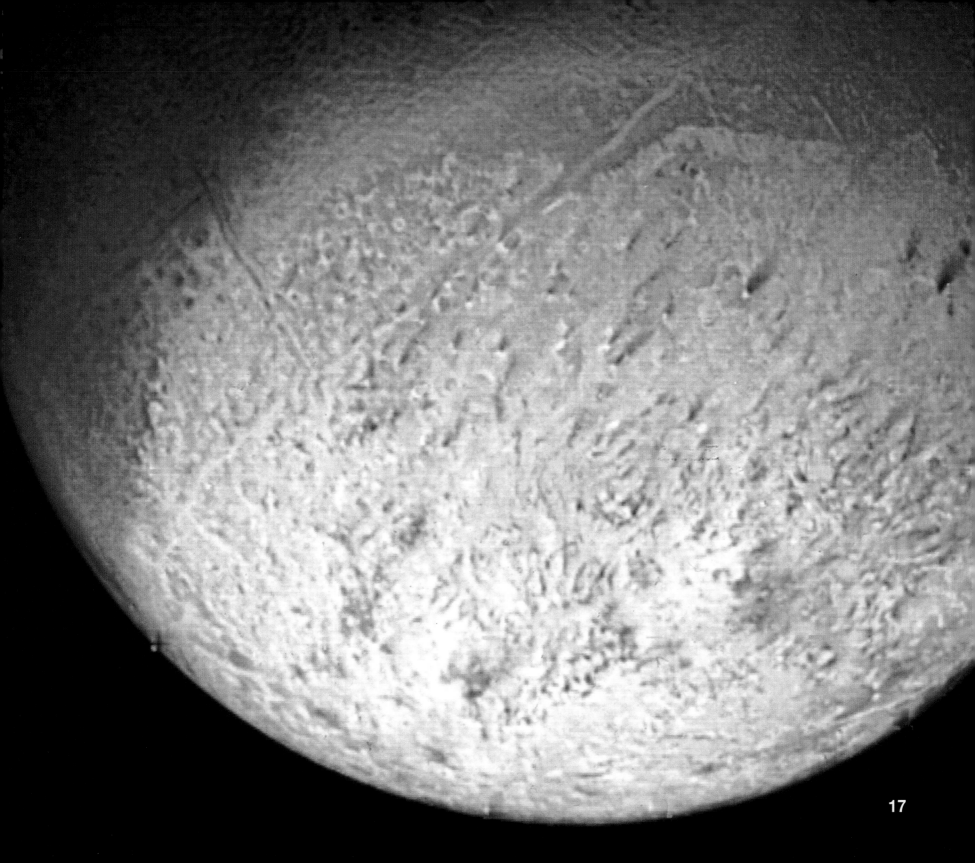

People and Neptune

Neptune does not have
a solid surface. People
could not live on Neptune.

La gente y Neptuno

Neptuno no tiene una
superficie sólida. La gente
no podría vivir en Neptuno.

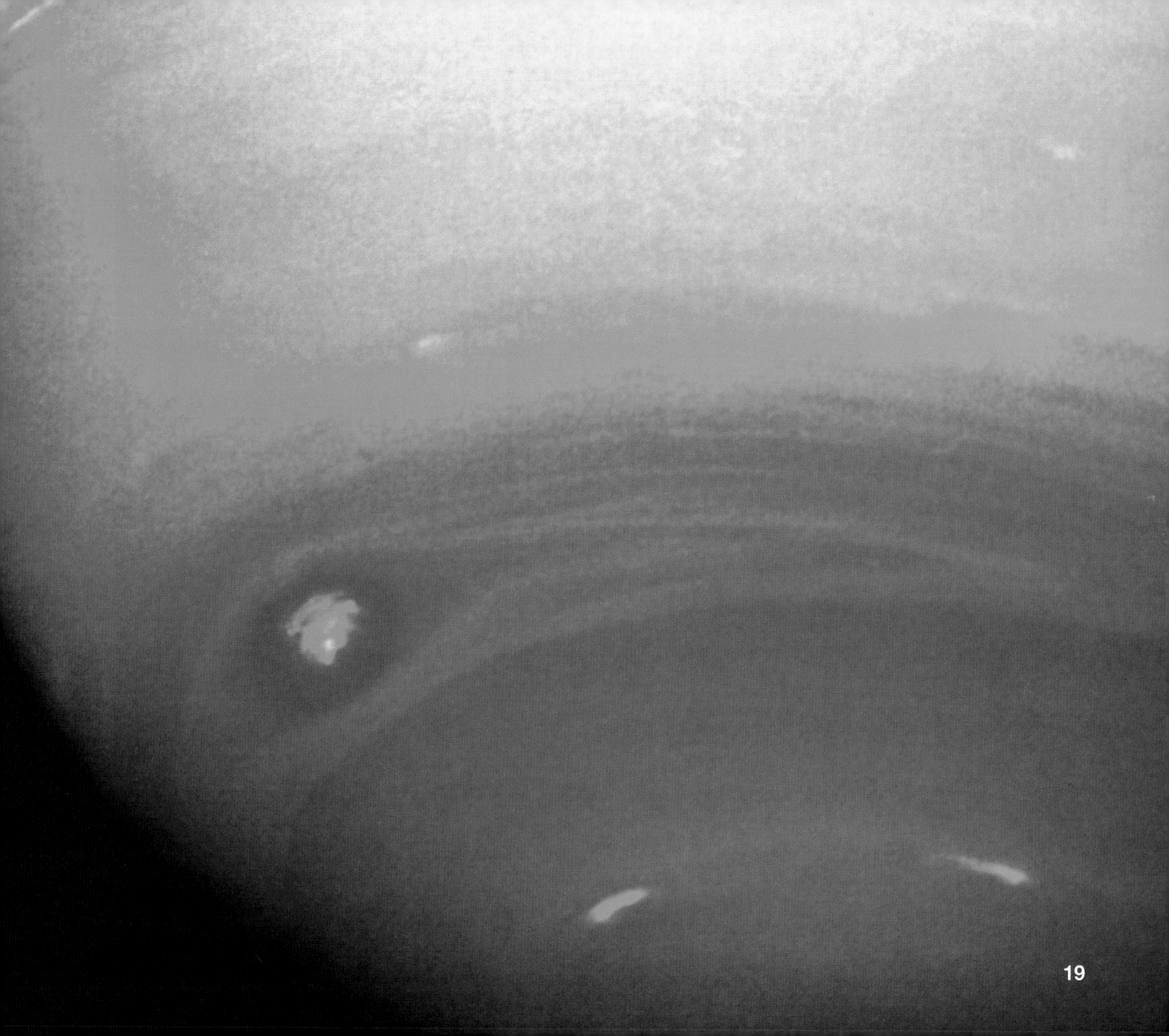

People cannot see Neptune
without a telescope. Neptune
is too far away.

La gente no puede ver a
Neptuno sin un telescopio.
Neptuno está demasiado lejos.

Glossary

gas—a substance, such as air, that spreads to fill any space that holds it; Neptune is called a gas giant; the other gas giants are Jupiter, Saturn, and Uranus.

moon—an object that moves around a planet

planet—a large object that moves around the Sun; Neptune is the eighth planet from the Sun.

Sun—the star that the planets move around; the Sun provides light and heat for the planets.

telescope—a tool people use to look at planets and other objects in space; telescopes make planets and other objects look closer than they really are.

Glosario

gas—una sustancia, como el aire, que se extiende hasta llenar el espacio que la contiene; a Neptuno se le conoce como un gigante gaseoso; los otros gigantes gaseosos son Júpiter, Saturno y Urano.

luna—un objeto que se mueve alrededor de un planeta

planeta—un objeto grande que se mueve alrededor del Sol; Neptuno es el octavo planeta a partir del Sol.

Sol—la estrella alrededor de la cual se mueven los planetas; el Sol proporciona luz y calor a los planetas.

telescopio—un instrumento que la gente usa para ver planetas y otros objetos en el espacio; los telescopios hacen que los planetas y otros objetos se vean más cerca de lo que están.

Internet Sites

Do you want to find out more about Neptune and the solar system? Let FactHound, our fact-finding hound dog, do the research for you.

Here's how:

1) Visit *www.facthound.com*

2) Type in the **Book ID** number: **0736821155**

3) Click on **FETCH IT**.

FactHound will fetch Internet sites picked by our editors just for you!

Sitios de Internet

¿Quieres saber más sobre Neptuno y el sistema solar? Deja que FactHound, nuestro perro sabueso, haga la investigación por ti.

Así:

1) Ve a *www.facthound.com*

2) Teclea el número ID del libro: **0736821155**

3) Clic en **FETCH IT**.

¡Facthound buscará en los sitios de Internet que han seleccionado nuestros editores sólo para ti!

Index

Índice